FOREWORD
By Mat and Pat

Pat and I grew up in the 1930s and ever since we were knee-high-to-a-grasshopper our Mommas told us there was two kinds of people: Those who went to church, and those who really should try to go to church more often. (That was called not being judgmental to the non-church-going folks 'cause God was the Judge and we weren't.) If you were exposed to only a part of church or just a touch of Christianity, church had the potential to seem rather odd and confusing. Misconceptions formed easily. Christians can seem more foreign than those bizarre Canadians.

We grew up in a small southern town where nearly everybody went to church. We never missed a Sunday. While the years went by, more and more folks started going less and less. They had their reasons. But Pat and I were raised to believe that you just don't stop going to church. Because of this, we have learned a whole lot about ourselves, our faith, and the world around us.

continued...

It dawned on us one Sunday afternoon as we were not working, or causing others to work, that there are a lot of people out there who continue to be confused about the church and have formed some odd opinions about Christianity. We wanted to help out. So, we put down our quilting and started to write this here book. Greg Scott drew some pictures every now and then to further explain our points. Thank you, Greg, for your accurate and educational drawings.

Humorist Mary Chambers once wrote that "Church is stranger than fiction." Pat and I agree. But we'd rather be strange and sitting in Church each Sunday morning than sitting at home watching Judge Wapner. For Pete's sake, the Lord gave you that fancy TiVo® so you can come to church and watch your favorite shows later!

Well now, it's time to make a casserole for Ladies Guild. Enjoy the book.

Mat and Pat

A cheerful heart is good medicine.

Proverbs 17:22 niv

5

If you think the four greatest apostles were John, Paul, George, and Ringo...

If you've never heard the joke, "Is this seat saved?" "No, but it's under conviction"...

...you may need to go to church more.

If you think "backsliding"
is something you do when
you fall down skiing...

...you may need to go to church
more and you may need to
stay on the Bunny Hill!

If you think the bishop in your church should only be able to walk diagonally...

...YOU MAY NEED TO GO TO CHURCH MORE.

If you think "Dedication Sunday" is when you get to ask the sound guy to play "You're the Inspiration" by Chicago for your sweetheart...

✝

...you may need to go to church more.

If you think Joan of Ark is Noah's wife...

...YOU MAY NEED TO GO TO CHURCH MORE.

If you think "leading someone to the throne" involves a flashlight and an outhouse...

...YOU MAY NEED TO
GO TO CHURCH MORE.

If you think "born again" is the sequel to the film "The Bourne Identity"...

...you may need to go to church more.

If you think being excommunicated means that your cell phone service has been interrupted...

...you may need to go
to church more.

If you think a "friar" is a position at a fast food restaurant...

...you may need to go to church more.

If you attempt to go for "seconds" during communion...

...YOU MAY NEED TO GO TO CHURCH MORE.

21

If you think the Great Crusades were back in the '70s when Billy Graham spoke in colosseums...

...you may need to go
to church more.

25

If you think Babylon
is what your pastor
tends to do...

...you may need to go to church more.

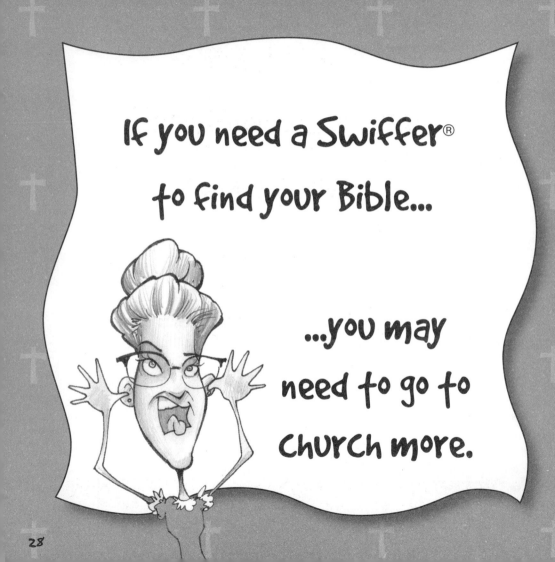

If you think the
"Great commission"
is a sales bonus...

...YOU MAY NEED TO GO TO CHURCH MORE.

If you sing the lyrics:
"We shall come rejoicing, bringing in the cheese," or "From the earth to the cross, my dead toupee"...

...you may need to
go to church more.

If you think a "revival meeting" is a CPR training course...

...you may need to go to church more.

If you think Calvinism simply means having really good taste in jeans...

...you may need to go to church more.

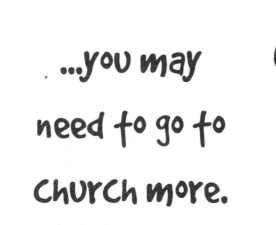

If instead of "Amen," you end your prayers with a very loud "Shazzam!!"...

...you may need to go to church more.

If the only thing you bring to a potluck dinner is a fork...

...you may need to go to church more.

If someone asks
you what denomination
you are affiliated with
and you tell them,
"Mostly large bills...
like 10s or 20s"...

...YOU MAY NEED TO GO TO CHURCH MORE.

If you are pretty sure
that the Popemobile
is mentioned in the
Old Testament...

...you may need to go to church more.

If you think the four great judges in the Bible were Joshua, Gideon, Samson, and Wapner...

...you may need to go to church more.

If you think "sacraments" are people from Northern California...

...you may need to go to church more.

If you think a
"Quaker meeting"
is where friends
go to eat oatmeal
together...

...you may need to go
to church more.

If your favorite Bible stories involve little pigs, blind mice, or itsy-bitsy spiders...

...you may need to go to church more.

If you haven't gotten any of the jokes in this book so far...

...YOU MAY NEED TO GO TO CHURCH MORE.

If you wish you could TiVo® church so you could fast forward through the sermon...

...you may need to go to church more.

If you think "original sin" means you found a creative way to do something wrong...

...you may need to go to church more.

If you think a

"roamin' catholic"

is a

sleep-walking

nun...

...you may need to go to church more.

If you think
Moody Bible Institute
is a clinic for emotionally
imbalanced christians...

...you may need to go
to church more.

If you think a "prophet"
is what you make on a
good deal...

...YOU MAY NEED TO GO TO CHURCH MORE.

If you think
"frankincense"
is a perfume
for monsters...

...you may need to go to church more.

If you think the saying "Life is like a box of chocolates" is from the Book of Proverbs...

...you may need to go to church more.

If you refer to church as that place where you go to play Bingo...

...you need to go to CHURCH RIGHT NOW!

If you think Mass is
"a fundamental property
of the object; a numerical
measure of its inertia;
a fundamental measure
of the amount of matter
in the object"...

...you may need to go
to church more...
and you're a lot
smarter than we are!

If you refer to going to church three Sundays in a row as a "turkey"...

...you may need to go to church more.

If you need to MapQuest® the directions to the church that you're a member of...

...YOU MAY NEED TO GO TO CHURCH MORE.

If your pastor refers to "shepherds" and "lost sheep" during his sermon and you're reminded of the "Dukes of Hazzard"...

...you may need to go to church more.

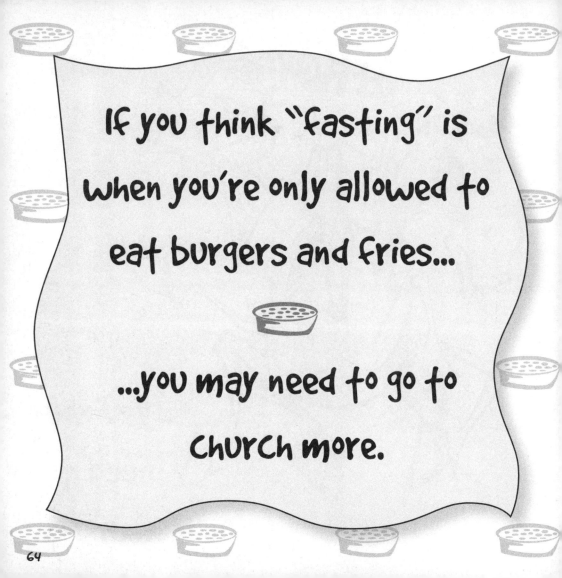

If you think "fasting" is when you're only allowed to eat burgers and fries...

...you may need to go to church more.

If you think Rumplestiltzkin was one of the kings of Israel...

...you may need to go to church more.

If you think canonizing
someone is what pirates
used to do...

...you may need to go
to church more.

Rrrrr

If you think a "parishioner" is someone who jumps out of an airplane...

†

...you may need to go to church more.

If your bath
towels have
the words
"Holiday Inn"
embroidered
onto them...

...YOU MAY NEED TO GO TO CHURCH MORE.

If you thought you learned all about the Reformation while watching "This old House"...

...you may need to go to church more.

If you thought "liturgy" had something to do with your ability to read...

...you may need to go to church more.

If you thought Pontius Pilot was a character on the TV show "CHiPs"...

...you may need to go to church more.

If your pastor
is talking about
paradise and you
suddenly crave a
cheeseburger...

...you may need to go
to church more.

If you refer to
John the Baptist
as
John the Lutheran...
✝
...you need to stop that!

If you have ever cheated on the entrance exam to get into Bible college...

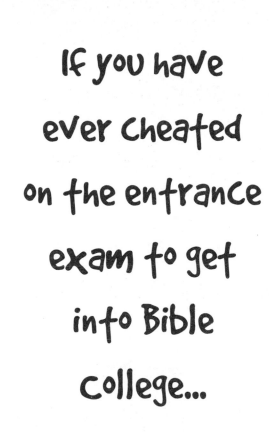

...YOU MAY NEED TO GO TO CHURCH MORE.

If you think a person who attends an evening service is called a Latter Day Saint...

...you may need to go to church more.

If you think "penance" is something you hope your baseball team wins...

...you may need to go to church more.

If you think that when you become a Christian you are instantly granted three wishes...

...you may need to go to church more.

If you think
2nd Chronicles
is "The Lion, the
Witch, and the
Wardrobe,
Part II"...

If the only time you've been in a confessional booth is by accident when you tried to vote...

✝

...you may need to go to church more.

If you make regular "guest" appearances on the TV show "COPS"...

...YOU MAY NEED TO GO TO CHURCH MORE.

If you refer to ushers
as "bouncers"...

...you may need to go to
church more.

If you think that the word "Maranatha" refers to a really, really long church service...

...you may need to go to church more.

If you think the
"Mark of the Beast"
is your crazy uncle's
tattoo...

...you may need to go to church more.

If you think the pulpit is that chunky stuff in orange juice...

...you may need to go to church more.

If you think the Book of Hebrews is about a man who makes coffee...

...YOU MAY NEED TO GO TO CHURCH MORE.

95

If you've ever asked the youth pastor why he wasn't a real pastor...

...you may need to go to church more.

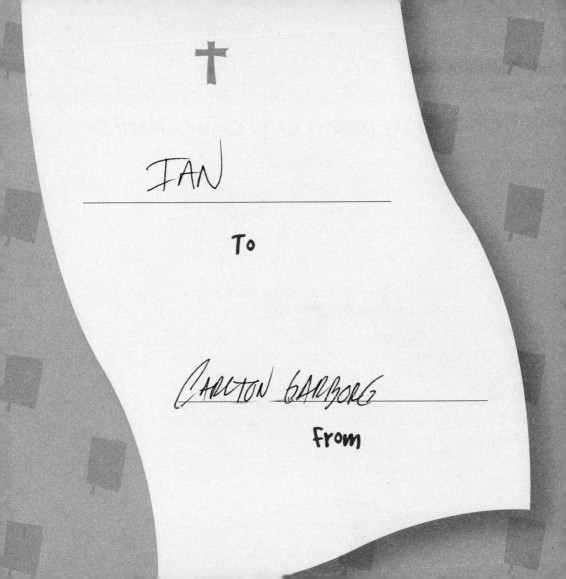

You May Need to Go to Church More...

Written by Mat and Pat*
Illustrated by Gregory A. Scott

Designed by Garborg Design Works

*Mat and Pat would like to thank Carlton Garborg and Richard DeJonge for their special contributions in writing this book.

ISBN 978-1-934770-44-3
Printed in USA